FIGURE STUDIES

D0720386

SOUTHERN MESSENGER POETS

Dave Smith, Series Editor

FIGURE STUDIES

POEMS

CLAUDIA EMERSON

LOUISIANA STATE UNIVERSITY PRESS

BATON ROUGE

Published by Louisiana State University Press
Copyright © 2008 by Claudia Emerson
All rights reserved
Manufactured in the United States of America
FIRST PRINTING

Designer: Barbara Neely Bourgoyne
Typeface: Quadraat
Printer and binder: Thomson-Shore, Inc.

Library of Congress Cataloging-in-Publication Data
Emerson, Claudia, 1957–
Figure studies : poems / Claudia Emerson.
    p. cm. — (Southern messenger poets)
    ISBN 978-0-8071-3360-6 (alk. paper) — ISBN 978-0-8071-3361-3 (pbk. : alk. paper)
    I. Title.
PS3551.N4155F54 2009
811'.54—dc22

2008007399

The author gratefully acknowledges the editors of the following periodicals, in which
some of the poems in this book have appeared previously, some in slightly different form:
Blackbird: "Esto Absoluta," "Headmaster," "Practice Rooms," "Synchronized Swimming," "The
Well: Egg and Tongue"; Cave Wall: "After the Affair," "Cat Lady," "Old Proof" (as "Hoarder");
Cincinnati Review: "Anatomical Model," "The Girls Dissect the Eye of a Cow," "Housemother,"
"Influenza," "Warmbloods"; Cortland Review: "Photographer"; Georgia Review: "Maintenance";
Greensboro Review: "Beginning Sculpture: The Subtractive Method," "Fire Drill," "The Physical
Plant" (as "The Physical Plant as Prologue"); Louisville Review: "Elevator Operator, Davnille,
Virginia, 1964" (as "Elevator Operator"), "Finger of Mercury"; Poetry: "Environmental
Awareness: The Right Whale," "Great Depression Story," "Physical Education," "Reunion
Weekend," "What They Are Missing"; Poetry East: "Latin Teacher"; Redivider: "Living Nativity,"
"Orchid Anatomy," "Upper Arcade"; Shenandoah: "Biology Lesson," "Communion Sunday
Buffet," "History Lesson," "Organist"; Southern Review: "Funny Valentine," "The Mannequin
above Main Street Motors"; Virginia Quarterly Review: "Anorexic, Farmers' Market," "The Medical
Venus," "Piano Fire," "The Polio Vaccine, Chatham, Virginia, 1964," "Spring Ice Storm";
Visions International: "What They Want."

"The Medical Venus" owes its inspiration and alludes to Georges Didi-Huberman's essay
"Wax Flesh, Vicious Circles" in Encyclopaedia Anatomica (Taschen, 1999).

The paper in this book meets the guidelines for permanence and durability of the Com-
mittee on Production Guidelines for Book Longevity of the Council on Library Resources.
∞

For my mother, Mollie Emerson

CONTENTS

II. GOSSIPS

III. EARLY LESSONS

IV.

ACKNOWLEDGMENTS

I want to thank the friends, colleagues, and fellow poets who helped me along the way with this book: my husband, Kent Ippolito; Betty and Don Adcock; Michael Bibler; Carole Garmon; Jim Groom; Sarah Kennedy; Meghan Gehman Holub; Eric Lorentzen; Tim McBride; Marie McAllister; Danny and Linda Marion; Buffy Morgan; Debra Nystrom; Alyson Poska; Amanda Rutstein; Mara Scanlon; Allison Seay; Dave Smith; Rod Smith; Laura-Gray Street; and a special thanks to Bruce Dalzell, who burned a piano for me on the banks of the Hocking River in Athens, Ohio, so I could conduct research.

FIGURE STUDIES

The Mannequin above *Main Street Motors*

When the only ladies' dress shop closed,
she was left on the street for trash, unsalvageable,

one arm missing, lost at the shoulder, one leg
at the hip. But she was wearing a blue-sequined negligee

and blonde wig, so they helped themselves to her
on a lark—drunken impulse—and for years kept her

leaning in a corner, beside an attic
window, rendered invisible. The dusk

was also perpetual in the garage below,
punctuated only by bare bulbs hung close

over the engines. An oily grime coated
the walls, and a decade of calendars promoted

stock-car drivers, women in dated swimsuits,
even their bodies out of fashion. Radio distorted

there; cigarette smoke moaned, the pedal steel
conceding to that place a greater, echoing

sorrow. So, lame, forgotten prank, she remained,
back turned forever to the dark storage

behind her, gaze leveled just above
anyone's who could have looked up

to mistake in the cast of her face fresh longing—
her expression still reluctant figure for it.

I

ALL GIRLS SCHOOL

Thus the object of secluding women at menstruation is to neutralize the dangerous influences which are supposed to emanate from them at all such times. That the danger is believed to be especially great at the first menstruation appears from the unusual precautions taken to isolate girls at this crisis. Two of these precautions have been illustrated above, namely, the rules that girls may not touch the ground nor see the sun. The general effect of these rules is to keep her suspended, so to say, between heaven and earth. Whether enveloped in her hammock and slung up on the roof, as in South America, or raised above the ground in a dark and narrow cage, as in New Ireland, she may be considered to be out of the way of doing mischief, since, being shut off both from the earth and from the sun, she can poison neither of these great sources of life by her deadly contagion. In short, she is rendered harmless by being, in electrical language, insulated.

Sir George Frazer, *The Golden Bough: A Study in Magic and Religion*

Ranged on benches down the sides of the room, the eighty girls sat motionless and erect: a quaint assemblage they appeared, all with plain locks combed from their faces, not a curl was visible. . . . [I]t suited them ill, and gave an air of oddity even to the prettiest.

Charlotte Brontë, *Jane Eyre*

The Physical Plant

Everything here measures: weight, effort, sin—
and everything costs in this seclusion

of daughters—the place an ark, its hold
all of a kind in an archaic, combed

order: straightened teeth, trained spines, the chapel's
benches in rigid rows before crimson

kneeling pillows, slim beds in dormitories,
the muted ticking of practice rooms, horses' stalls

just-mucked, the halls humid with breathing.
And in the brushes, their hair—enough to line

the nests of a hundred generations of birds.

Headmaster

He rocks up onto the balls of his feet,
clears his throat to lead the assembly

with a voice more familiar than their fathers',
brothers', those distant as only kin can be. The girls

surround him, the youngest sitting on the floor, close
enough to notice in his loafers the clean,

empty slits where the pennies are supposed to go.

Housemother

This life began as mere employment, something
that would pass; she had private joys then,

reasons to close her door. This is how she breathes
now, moving sharklike through the halls' courses,

sensing the constant blood of wakefulness,
girls' hands swimming—pale fish—into and out of tense

bodies held still as water dense with early blooming.

Anatomical Model

They have retired her, alongside turtles'
shells, bees' nests, and the skeletons of birds,

to a narrow glass closet. She is antique
but not inaccurate—headless, armless,

all torso, a sculpture mutilated. The breast
lifts off, easy as the lid from a pot, the heart

and lungs beneath; the belly comes away then
from neat intestines, from the chalky fetus nestled

in the womb worn smooth from all the hands
reaching in for this conclusion.

The Girls Dissect the Eye of a Cow

They gather around it, bored or enthralled
in the aqueous chamber, center of the blind

spot, pupil, iris. It has been released
from its orbit, from the body's confinement,

the sullen, perpetual cud, fence line, salt lick
and sun, from long nights spent wading in ruminant

fog. They cannot reconcile themselves
with this thing intent on them, whether

eye of the wind, the needle, or heaven.

Latin Teacher

Seamed stockings, sensible shoes, cardigan
buttoned all the way to the top, she greets

each of them by name as they enter her classroom
rebellious, identical. They want Italian,

French, a younger teacher—anything
but this woman fluent in a language

that will not travel—the deep south of her vowels
slow as the minute hand on the grinding clock

behind her. Her hair is braided and coiled, contained
in a bun substantial as a hornets' nest—ashen gray.

But their mothers also were made to take it—
translations all the more hated for being inherited.

Then they are assigned to her table in the din
of the dining room, where she directs them

to eat even popsicles with a knife and fork.
She serves fried chicken by inquiring if they prefer

to *walk* or *fly*. And they learn to choose the leaner wing
because they believe it pleases her. At Halloween,

in the darkened gymnasium, beside the tub of water
where girls bob for apples, she sits in a small

booth to tell fortunes, peers into their palms:
esto perpetua, whispering again

and again the same lie of a life so long
they don't listen—their attentions lost

instead in the swung shock of her hair
let down into luminescence, brushing the floor

like a curtain just closing behind her.

Beginning Sculpture: The Subtractive Method

They sit before the assignment—identical
blocks of salt—and from tall, precarious stools,

look down into blank planes of possibility. In the end,
though, the only choice is to carve something

smaller. So they begin. Rough chunks like hail
fall before the rasps' and chisels' beveled

edges. Salt permeates this air as it has
for years, the floor gritty, their hands, eyes,

even the skylights made opaque with it—
disappearing not unlike the way it is

subtracted from similar blocks, in the fields,
before the tongues of the horses.

Warmbloods

Tails, manes, and forelocks painstakingly braided,
they have submitted all afternoon to the saddle—

the bit's dull, metallic taste. Now, outside
the close, dark stalls—hay fragrant in the loft above—

they hold still for hard, sharp blasts of water,
bodies steaming, shuddering beneath last,

dutiful brushes. Thousand-pound creatures,
generations broken, their only wildness is this

ninety pounds of girl—hard hat of velvet
veneer, heels neatly down, the controlled, meant

growl behind the ear before the jump. Tonight
while the girls sleep, they will be allowed the fog-white

pasture, where the deer, unafraid of sharing
this fate, seek the careful grass and easier salt—

and the warmbloods will roll on their backs, the joy
of the earth behind them, hooves loosed, pounding soundless sky.

What They Are Missing

The local boys are, of course, forbidden.
This leaves only the rare visiting

father, awkward brother, the headmaster,
the boy who bushhogs the pasture,

or the chaplain in his telling collar—starched
tooth at the throat—to remind them.

Living Nativity

They have filled roles from Willie Loman to Lear,
from Atticus Finch to the Gentleman Caller,

convincing themselves and each other that they are
to be believed. So now as the innkeeper,

Joseph, the kings, and shepherds—charcoal-bearded—
they have rehearsed their easy entrances,

when and how to kneel, where to place the myrrh
and frankincense. But the virgin is always

a secret until the last hour, her identity known
only by the headmaster, who has chosen her,

and the housemother, who whisks away the prettiest
from the candlelit Christmas banquet

to brush her already-brushed hair and drape her
in della robbia blue—made soft by years

of other girls. She is placed as they were
center stage where a spotlight reveals her

gazing marblelike into the manger—nothing
for her to know beyond the fact of being

chosen, nothing for her to practice,
having learned already this stillness.

Organist

They know he doesn't want them—and love him for it.
His hair uncut, uncombed, all his clothes worn soft,

he is thoughtless about the body he inhabits,
and they are part of his denial of it.

They line up around the chapel for the year's
audition, desperate to be chosen for the choir,

where they learn the proper way to open their mouths
and breathe, wear the crimson-collared robes,

and ascend the dim spiral of stairs into the loft.
He entices a few to study the guitar or flute—

slim, bright, divisible—says the organ
is a jealous thing, selfish as God to demand

he come to it in this ornate house where he is
always cold and the leaded glass casts

dim, rose-gold translations of light. Yet, long after
the last bell, they will listen to his sustaining practice,

sleep-confusing music, uncontainable as desire.

Communion Sunday Buffet

It is the same every month, the steamship
of beef slow cooked; they have breathed it

all day—and have grown sick of it. At the toll
of the bell, though, they line up in church-formal

dresses before gold-rimmed plates of creamy
porcelain emptiness. His apron bloody,

he holds on to the handle of the exposed
shankbone to slice the lean-muscled meat across

its grain. They'd prefer the salad but cannot
bear disappointment in him, who has worked

all his Sunday for them. So, his carving knife
poised beside the bright tines of the serving fork,

they hold out their plates to him, and, for the second
time this day, offer up their patient tongues.

The Well: Egg and Tongue

Each day before the bell sounds the noon meal,
they lounge on the main staircase. The stairwell

rises into a great dome, voices listing
upward and lingering in it with mothlike

aimlessness—while, at the base of the well, an antique
pattern repeats itself in alabaster measure,

the endless egg and tongue soothing, voiceless.

Upper Arcade

In the brief hour that spans study hall and bed,
the girls—already nightgowned, barefoot—are allowed

to move between buildings on the high, narrow walkway
that couples the dormitories at the second story.

Supported from beneath by a sequence
of vaulted arches, the arcade frees them

to open air, and sometimes they lean out as though over
the railing of a ship, wind shushing the waxy clatter

of the magnolias. Or, though warned not to, they run
back and forth, lightly defiant, leaping up and up

to land quietly, spines arched as they have been taught
in dance class, the hand-polished barre and long

mirrored wall where they watched themselves learn this
now forgotten, locked in the reflection of darkness beneath them.

Biology Lesson

It seems impossible that there could be
any ancestral link between the turtle—

plodding, benevolent creature they keep
in a glass terrarium—and any bird,

but once the teacher suggests it, they begin to see—
in the blunt beak stained with mulberry juice,

the low brow, eyes, the scales on its legs—certain,
if, at first, strained resemblance. Then, even

in its poor posture, they are convinced of another
sky into which it withdraws, not to become

invisible, but to soar, fearless, inside
itself—small dome of safe, starless heaven.

Orchid Anatomy

This evening's study the anatomy of the orchid,
the greenhouse glows—jut of glass at the third story

of the science building—a small, tended jungle
thriving in its humid room. Wearing identical

lab aprons, they lean over the misting table
or peer into the daintier air-orchids

in order to name and sketch the parts,
committing to memory the sepals, inner whorl

of petals, the column where male and female
fuse, and the sticky, stigmatic surface

of the pouting lip where birds, moths,
and bees would land if allowed this sterile

world. Each wall, even the vaulted roof
a canvas, all their breathing dissolves

into the ordered atmosphere of this
one sustained season—until, if seen

from the outside, the glass's weeping would
render them recognizable but changed,

their bodies, braids, aprons, the green leaves running
into a pleasing, impressionistic bleed.

Influenza

To it, fertile as gossip, this is a thick,
crowded seed-plot of the easiest

exposures; each month opens and closes
already in the quiet synchrony of their bodies.

They turn in fevered beds, the infirmary overrun.
To the one nurse, pale as her apron,

all is suspect—doorknobs, washcloths, glass rims,
even the surely sterile thermometer, mercury

rising under each new tongue. Invisible knife
they will have gone under, it sharpens itself

in them and will pass on, convalescence
coming behind it, balmy, shared as weather.

Practice Rooms

Plastic cubicles line the long fluorescent
hallway—clear cells hardened into soundlessness;

each contains a piano, metronome, one girl.
The isolations partial by design,

the proctor watches hands obey prescribed
measures, a body's particular sway, head

moving in concentration—music immured behind
the pierced lobe, sculpted whorl of auricle, the temporal bone.

Physical Education

The hockey coach travels to the field
in a golf cart rattled with whistles,

rackets, sticks, and cleats. And from behind
the wheel, she metes out laps like lashes; terrified,

they circle the school the way water, not yet
furious, trains around an impatient

drain: run—*you girls, you stupid, stupid girls.*

Synchronized Swimming

Prim noseclips firmly in place, hair molded,
bunned at the nape, even muscle groups schooled

into exact definitions, one body appears
cloned. Linked arm to shoulder, a female strand,

the team enters the pool supple as an otter
flowing from a river-smooth rock to gather

itself into the first of the ornamental
formations. For this, they have land-drilled—

practicing poolside when and how to move,
breathe, even their smiles choreographed.

Upside-down now to assume the vertical figure,
stillness is as much part of this execution

as motion. Hands fluttering, the scull supports
legs scissoring the air before they close,

plunging into the shimmering screen of water.
The girls' disappearance so quick, precise,

the surface tension barely perceives the clean
incisions—before they reappear with ease:

bright fragments inside a kaleidoscope
dialing inflorescent patterns of glass.

Environmental Awareness: The Right Whale

The whale was known as *right* because it was
magnificent with oil, slow and easy

to find and slaughter, floating even when dead.
But after it was no longer needed for fat,

men still hunted the whale for its rich mouth
of baleen, harvested for hairbrushes,

buggy whips, umbrella ribs, the stays
of corsets—vain things designed to mold the female

body, sculpt a waist so small a man's
hands could meet with ease around it. Crazy,

the girls agree, the way those women bought it.

History Lesson

They have been half-listening to a lecture
on the Great Depression when the teacher

looks up, begins to talk about the president
and trout fishing—a digression, he admits,

that will not be on the test. Hoover would
catch too many trout to eat and so had

a small cement pool constructed; he'd keep
the fish for days while he calmly read at the edge

of the water, absentmindedly hand-feeding
them beefhearts brought in from Washington

as though to tame them. Later, the girls
can think of nothing else, circling the goldfish

pond, throwing bits of a dinner roll onto the surface,
the fish rising to them through water so still

their slow refusal to school is its only motion.

.

Esto Absoluta

Despite the hallway lined with a hundred years
of girls framed in graduation white,

they can allow themselves to imagine the detritus
of classrooms, laboratories—beakers and vials—

mingling with leaf dust, and wasps passing
unhurried through the windows' paneless grid

to nest in the halls' mute bells. Rain comes in,
snow, then slower ivy in dusky air. Pigeons,

ubiquitous, whose placid voices have long
accompanied such dreaming, enter their rooms

as though enrolled, resigned to the girls' fate,
to the blackboard's chalky refusals—latent equations,

declensions, proofs—all their failed erasures.

Fire Drill

Bells sound them from sleep, and their imaginations
rise, recite all they have been told: the curtains

on fire, the beds, nightgowns, their hair, their hair.
They've practiced this escape before

and know to close the windows last, descend
the ringing flights of stairs in perfect wordlessness

to line up, barefoot, on the dew-wet lawn,
face the building, pretend to watch it burn.

Reunion Weekend

Thirty years later, drunk on red wine, they will return
to wander the halls searching for a certain

room, its window still memorized—will delight
in finding through familiar panes the moon rising

just the way it had when they'd lain sleepless
beneath it. But they cannot return to the twin bed,

long assigned, reassigned to some other
possibility sick for home, another

disappointment—the room itself practicing
what they will have come to prove cannot be finished.

II

GOSSIPS

"Dammit sir," Judge Stevens said, "will you accuse a lady to her face of smelling bad?"

William Faulkner, "A Rose for Emily"

Funny Valentine

She had been a late and only child to parents
already old and set; none of us had ever

wanted to go inside that hushed house
and play with her, her room too neat, doll-crowded.

We did encourage her later, though, to enter
the high school talent contest—after we'd heard

her singing *My Funny Valentine* in a stall
in the girls' bathroom, reckoning the boys

would laugh, perhaps find us even prettier
in comparison. Still, we would not have predicted

those wisteria-scaled walls, the one room
we could see from the street with its windows

open year round so that greening vines entered
and birds flew in and out—*bad luck*, we thought,

bad luck. By then we were members of the ladies'
garden club, the condition of her house

and what had been its garden a monthly
refreshment of disappointment, the most

delectable complaint her parents' last
Coupe de Ville sinking in tangled orchard grass

and filled to the roof—plush front seat and rear—
with paperbacks, fat, redundant romances

she had not quite thrown away—*laughable,*
we laughed, *unphotographable*—with wild restraint.

Anorexic, Farmers' Market

All around her, we sounded melons, practiced
at hearing what we couldn't see, pretending not

to notice when she stopped at the stall where the Amish
displayed their loaves of zucchini and pumpkin bread,

hand-thick oatmeal cookies, pecan pies,
all wrapped in plastic, airless, preserving.

Touching the invisible film, she looked
as though she were trying to choose—or touch

some part of herself, her own skin paling,
illusory, her hair falling water-thin

and colorless behind her. We had seen
her denial before, backward hoarding,

the house emptied except the dark cellar
where she'd put up the sterile breath of resolve

in jars, wax-sealed, ordered, a reversal
that deliberate, and that much work.

We were relieved when she chose at last
red bell peppers to weigh in the scale's basket

hung beneath its palsied needle, then counted
exact change from her zippered purse. We watched

her leaving, disappearing behind a line
of brightly painted gourds swinging, opened

and hollowed for birds to nest inside,
perfect round mouths vine-chased, filled with wind.

Old Proof

Sometimes we saw her on the junk-burdened
porch, her body long indistinguishable

from its house. If she acknowledged us,
it was with a wave that said go on, *go on,*

she was fine. The man who serviced the furnace
told us she'd saved at least thirty years' worth

of catalogs, phone books, newspapers—walls
lost behind thick stacks rising to the ceilings—

that the smell was of damp paper and ink and that throughout
the soundless house, all she'd left herself were the strictest

of paths, like a worm's slow maze through those words
she kept, old proof of us, our crowded world.

What They Want

> They covet fields and seize them; and houses, and take them away.
> Micah 2:2

1

The men faked a collective boredom, nodded, spat,
bid—and would buy it all divided: pasture,

tractor, flatbed, bulkbarns—then the house
where the auctioneer called, convincing us

to bid for all we had desired, had coveted
all those years: her hats would go for one money—

felt, fur, straw, the velvet one from which the feathers
of an egret rose white and trembled, as though her head

still turned to nod to us. He would make us admit it,
make us wear what she wore, what yet bore her favorite scent,

what we had sworn beneath the preacher's drone,
hissing, we would not be caught dead in.

2

The story had its way with us the way a bee bores first
into the mouth of one rose and then another: *they found her*

where how many days my word my God the coffin closed
of course can you imagine how sad she died alone, we said, how sad.

By the time we saw the doll wheeled out in its carriage, wicker-white,
it might as well have been her heart cradled, still warm. Held high

above us like a long-awaited heir—old, infant—she delighted us.
The bidding climbed, an aberrant vine, as the doll cried out

her one vowel, eyes opening, then closing inside the perfect
form of her face.—Oh, what we wouldn't give for her.

III

EARLY LESSONS

"I'm little but I'm old," he said.

Harper Lee, *To Kill a Mockingbird*

The Polio Vaccine, Chatham, Virginia, 1964

For Inez Shields

It was not death we learned to fear but her life,
her other birth, waking remade from the womb

of that disease. One leg was withered, a dragging-
numb weight behind her, one shoulder humped—

a camel's—and what did we know of that foreign
beast but ugliness and that she carried in it hard

faith like water. And so we did what we were told:
outside the elementary school, the long line drowsed.

We saw gleaming trays of sugar cubes rose-pink
with the livid virus tamed, its own undoing.

We opened our mouths, held it on our tongues
and, as with any candy, savored the sharp corners

going, the edges, until at last the form gave way
to grain, to sweet sand washing against the salt of us.

Cat Lady

Ours was a widow, childless. We knew she wore
that bathrobe in the daytime, smoked Camels, and drove

the flat-black Pontiac that had grown old with her.
And we knew about the cats. When we came to deliver

her groceries, or rake leaves, we could see
through her back door: they were perched on the pie safe,

the refrigerator, the kitchen table—shadow-
quiet, watchful as owls at dusk. And the smell

was not just of cat piss and foul tinned fish
but of something more—the heat of cats' yawning,

an old woman's long and smoky hair. We could never
describe it—and could not help imagining

out of that quiet the sound of urgent nursing
from glistening knots of newborn kittens,

the wail and hiss of mating, dying, the beat of all those hearts.

Piano Fire

How she must have dreaded us and our sweaty coins,
more than we hated practice, the lessons,

scales, the winter-hot parlor, arthritic
hands, the metronome's tick. She lectured

to us about the history of the piano:
baby and concert grand, spinet and player

had come across oceans in the holds of ships,
across continents in mule-drawn wagons,

heavier than all the dead left behind. On her face
we could see the worry: the struggle had come to this,

the black upright she had once loved haunting
the room it could never leave. And her piano

was now one of a mute, discordant population
doomed to oldfolks homes, bars, church basements,

poolhalls, funeral parlors—or more mercifully
abandoned on back porches where at least

chickens could nest, or the cat have kittens.
So when she could no longer play well enough

even to teach us, she hired some of the men
to haul out and burn the piano in the field behind

the house. We watched the keys catch, furious, and all
at once, heard in the fire a musiclike relief

when the several tons of tension let go, heat
becoming wind on our faces. We learned that

when true ivory burns the flame is playful,
quick, and green. And in the ash, last lessons:

the clawed brass feet we had never before noticed,
the harp's confusion of wire, and the pedals we'd worn

thin, shaped like quenched-hard tongues—loud, soft,
sustain. We waited with her until they were cool enough to touch.

Elevator Operator, Danville, Virginia, 1964

All day she ferried them—almost all
women, all white—as they rose to fall

in strict passage, the gondola close to airlessness,
curfew-dark. She filled the forward corner, perched

on a small, fold-down stool from which she could
reach with ease both the lever and the collapsing

metal lattice of the door. All day she closed
them in like perfumed birds rustling nylons,

shopping bags, purses—and released them again
to the few destinations she had to repeat, announcing:

third floor—men's wear, mezzanine—unseen steel
cables controlling all of them in endless,

storied looping. Only children saw her until
most learned not to, looking up instead to the dial

above the door, its face an eclipsed compass,
the ornate brass needle of her voice

sweeping east to west to east by the northern
route—as though the south were never there.

Finger of Mercury

She said we were the usual ones to ask,
despite our mothers' hushing, and wished

she had a better story to tell. But truth
was, she'd been hot one late afternoon,

the sun bare in a cloudless sky, and the pool was closed,
surrounded by a chain-link fence she climbed

with ease. But when she dropped to the other side,
the little finger from her left hand refused,

gravity delivering her of it
with only the slightest resistance.

She felt betrayed when she looked up, saw it
hanging there, lost easily as a tooth,

or a skink's tail. There was no pain at first,
numb blood, and what else was there to do but

climb back up and get it? She drove herself
to the clinic, finger tissue-swaddled, mute infant

too small to save—two joints, a ragged nail,
the whorl of print already failing

evidence of her. The surgeon couldn't
reattach it, but neatened the wound,

fashioning a small, pale flap like an envelope's.
So she placed it in a matchbox and buried it

in the garden next to the cat, telling herself
she wouldn't miss the finger half as much.

And yet her body insisted ever since
on recalling it—with phantom itch, the ache of arthritis

in the bone so real she could, even now, wake
in the morning surprised to find it gone—good

reminder, she said, that she could suffer worse,
a blessing, really, any lesson in smaller loss.

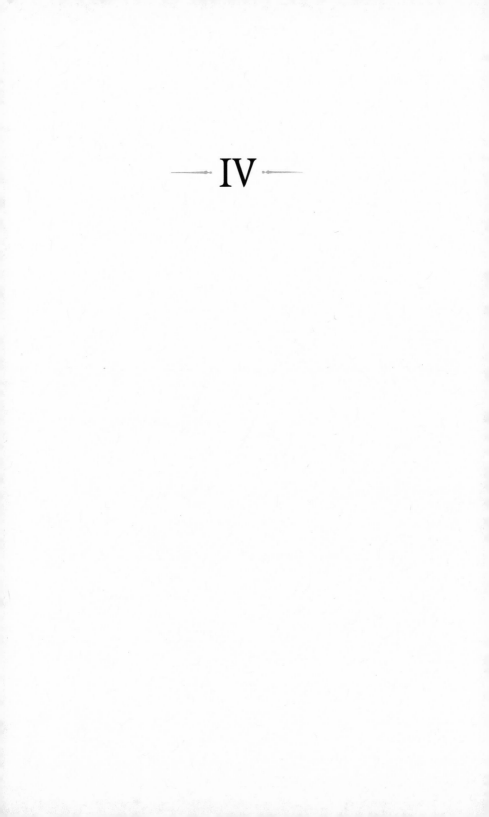

IV

Triptych

AFTER THE AFFAIR

There was no one to tell it to, so the guilt
settled in the lines of the house, in sills,

doorframes, ceilings. In the late afternoons
that followed, she heard what could have been someone

knocking, the cardinal beating its body against
the living room window as though desperate

to come inside. It could not see the space
beyond the glass, or know that it had been deceived

again into mistaking itself for something else.
At dusk, when the windows' slow reversal

released it, turning instead to her own face, disfamiliar,
terrible, she also knew the same desire

to fly into that room, that house, some other woman.

STUDIO

She had said she needed this, and time,
to write, and often she had written here, the room

almost bare: only a desk beneath
tall, thin windows, a lamp, loveseat,

a dictionary the wind browsed—all sentient
with waiting. Then, when she could not abandon

the lie, grief became its sharper part, secreted
into the hours she was still obligated

to come here—the long mirror where she had
admired herself returning the pale gray

of a shadowless wall. The typewriter old, anchor-
heavy, she began again—filling sheet after

sheet with drafts she would abandon, the black
ribbon of ink spooling vowels, words, ragged

lines away from her in pale relief, her head
bowed beneath curtains so sheer they might have been

meaningless except in giving form
to the wind, when there was one.

THE GARDEN

She made her husband's dinner in the afternoon,
then sealed it for him to warm up later while she gardened

well past dark. Used to it, he no longer complained.
Every morning she let in the neighbor's gray cat;

she didn't know his name, had never fed him,
but every day he returned, faithful, to spend

hours moving with the sun through her house in a drowsy
migration. Sometimes he followed her into the garden,

would rub against her legs as though comforting her,
as though he alone understood that every bulb she sank into this earth

was another stone sewn into the hem of her skirt.

Sewing Bird

Before the invention of the sewing machine, women used sewing
clamps to fix one end of a piece of cloth to a table, thus allowing
them to hold it taut with one hand while sewing with the other.
Even after the sewing machine rendered them obsolete, sewing
birds were given by men to their fiancées as betrothal gifts.

No bigger than the span of any woman's
hand, this one was cast in ornate brass,

even the thumb key, designed to clamp the bird
to the table's edge made decorative.

A small velvet cushion for needles
and pins wears like a prissy saddle,

and though the posture is of diving, or soaring,
wings out and back, its bill opened to hold

fast the cotton, wool, or muslin—rarer
lace—the stuff of the nest its gag: trousers,

aprons, christening gown—a wedding dress's
seams felled so perfectly the inside was

as flawless as the out. Where the syrinx
nestled, warm song chamber inside the body

of any living bird that might have sung
outside the window, spring steel still recalls

the stricture of its hidden coil, a singular
memory. Its strength in such closure,

the mouth shut to the finished task—the bird's
only lyric measured and cut to be worn,

torn, mended, and handed down—soundless
cloth the swaddling of yet another's voice.

Photographer

It began with the first baby, the house
disappearing threshold by threshold, rooms

milky above the floor only her heel,
the ball of her foot perceived. The one thing real

was the crying; it had a low ceiling
she ducked beneath—but unscalable walls.

Then she found with the second child
a safer room in the *camera obscura*, handheld,

her eye to them a petaled aperture,
her voice inside the dark cloth muffled

as when they first learned it. Here, too, she steadied,
stilled them in black and white, grayscaled the bee-stung

eye, the urine-wet bedsheet, vomit, pox,
pout, fever, measles, stitches fresh-black,

bloody nose—the expected shared mishap
and redundant disease. In the evenings

while they slept, she developed the day's film
or printed in the quiet darkroom, their images

under the enlarger, awash in the stop bath,
or hanging from the line to dry. Sometimes

she manipulated their nakedness, blonde hair
and bodies dodged whiter in a mountain stream

she burned dark, thick as crude oil or tar. The children's
expressions fixed in remedial reversals,

she sleeved and cataloged them, her desire,
after all, not so different from any other mother's.

At the Route One Flea Market

Inside makeshift stalls, hawkers slumped in
resigned habit, their tables weighted down

with everything broken—fans, dolls, blenders,
clocks—all destined for the trash heap, suspended—

spared—for at least one more late Saturday afternoon.
To the side and behind them, a lone structure

listed, small as a bedroom—or a circus wagon
stalled at the edge of a field shrinking

toward it. She was its door, set in the blank
wooden frame, old clearly, swaddled in blankets

mummylike, diminishing inward
as though packed with mud and lichen,

her body given over to that kind of waiting.
Three ragged Xs painted black on a cardboard sign

told what she was selling besides some chipped
dishes and empty picture frames: boxes

of magazines and tapes surrounded her,
crowding the shaded space of the room behind her,

all of it handled, wound and rewound, all
those dated, glossed bodies used past desire. Still,

she'd gesture, call out, when anyone wandered
near: *If there's one thing I can't never keep in here,*

it's them pictures—fingering in her patient
lap the small purse, its emptiness worried soft.

Womanless Beauty Pageant at the
Volunteer Fire Department

It was cheap and easy to pull off, the men
scouring their wives' chests of drawers and closets

for knee-highs, garter belts, brassieres, petticoats,
and bathing suits—anything made from polyester,

spandex, anything with *give* at the waist,
before sending their wives to the Goodwill for wigs

and high heels. Just before the show, the women
would make them up, tickling with blush, eyeliner,

and lipstick, heavy on the reds and pinks.
Deliberately talentless, then, they sang

and danced, paraded on the makeshift stage
they'd built in the firehouse, baring veined,

coquettish legs, hairy bellies—the audience
hysterical, the women's laughter rising

past mere amusement despite themselves, despite
the restless *what on earth* these men had put on,

those dresses they'd rather burn than wear again.

Maintenance

He lit the pilot lights of a town full
of widows living alone in bedrooms

off the kitchens of hulking houses built
by dead men, houses shrugging off paint with rain,

rain with years. He bellied through crawl spaces,
eased down rotting ladders, humped stairs

to each widow's core, her every fall's concern:
her furnace. He had blocked ducts to libraries,

living rooms, dining rooms, unused bedrooms
filled with faded canopies, empty highboys,

wardrobes, armoires of peeling veneer. Brittle vanities
shrank in the cold. He laid his head against

the bosom of one house and listened to a diminished
power equal to a lesser task. Satisfied,

he ducked under a sagging line of support stockings
that danced to dry heat, flicked off his flashlight,

and ascended to reassure one more woman with poor
circulation that as she slept one more winter

on her narrow bed beneath a borderless
puzzle of photographs, she would be warm.

Spring Ice Storm

The forecast had not predicted it,
and its beginning, a calming, rumbled dusk

and pleasant lightning, she welcomed as harbinger
of rain. Then as night came she heard the world

relapse, slide backward into winter's insistent
tick and hiss. In the morning, she woke to a powerless

house, the baseboards cold, the sky blank,
mercury hardfallen as the ice and fixed

even at noon. The woodpile on the porch dwindled
to its last layer; she had not replenished it

for a month and could see beyond it windblown ice
in the shed where the axe angled Excalibur-like,

frozen in the wood. Still, she didn't worry
beyond the fate of the daffodils, green-sheathed,

the forsythia and quince already bloomed out—
knowing this couldn't last. But by afternoon

she did begin feeding the fire in the cast-iron
stove ordinary things she thought she could replace,

watching through the small window of isinglass
the fast-burning wooden spoons, picture frames,

then the phone book and stack of old almanacs—
forgotten predictions and phases of the moon—

before resorting to a brittle wicker rocker,
quick as dried grass to catch, bedframes and slats,

ladderback chairs, the labor of breaking them up
against the porch railing its own warming.

Feverlike, the freeze broke after two days,
and she woke to a melting steady as the rain

had been. The fire she had tended more carefully
than the household it had consumed she could now

let go out, and she was surprised at how little
she mourned the rooms heat-scoured, readied for spring.

Great Depression Story

Sometimes the season changed in the telling,
sometimes the state, but it was always during

the Depression, and he was alone in the boxcar,
the train stalled beneath a sky wider

than any he'd seen so far, the fields of grass
wider than the sky. He'd been curious

to see if things were as bad somewhere else
as they were at home. They were—and worse,

he said, places with no trees, no water.
He hadn't eaten all day, all week, his hunger

hard-fixed, doubled, gleaming as the rails. A lone
house broke the sharp horizon, the train dreaming

beneath him, so he climbed down, walked out,
the grass parting at his knees. The windows

were open, curtainless, and the screendoor,
unlatched, moved to open, too, when he knocked.

He could see in all the way through to the kitchen—
and he smelled before he saw the lidded

pot on the stove, the steam escaping. Her clothes
moved on the line for all reply, the sheets,

a slip, one dress, washed thin, worn to translucence;
through it he could see what he mistook for fields

of roses until a crow flew in with the wind—
sudden, fleeting seam. By the time he got back to the train,

he'd guessed already what he'd taken—pot
and all—a hen, an old one that had quit

laying, he was sure, or she wouldn't have killed it.
The train began to move then, her house falling

away from him. The story ended with the meat
not quite done, but, believe him, he ate it

all, white and dark, back, breast, legs, and thighs,
strewing the still-warm bones behind him for miles.

The Medical Venus

The so-called Mediceische Venus is one of a collection of life-sized
anatomical wax models from the late eighteenth century. Designed
and used for teaching, she was created and is still kept at Museo La
Specola in Florence.

1

In the patient, quiet museum, she is exhibited
closed, indehiscent inside a glass casket,

reclining on her back, on hair long as her spine.
Her face is sublime as in the moment

before sleep, or after waking, eyes opening
or just closing, mouth barely parted as though

to draw a breath or speak, fine teeth suggested
behind the lasting red of her lips. A strand

of pearls encircles, defines her nakedness—
a luminescent sheen of shoulders, breasts,

and thighs—such wholeness a molded disremembrance
of what it took to make her, the wax itself

long removed from the hive's hexagonal prisms,
the cooling fan of temporal wings.

2

She is the house with a wall that removes
to a methodical inner progression

past seven layers—from pearls to rosy lungs,
to the great vessels that enter and leave

the heart, to the pelvic inlet where the fetus,
too, can be lifted out, serene, instructive.

3

On their way from sickbed to cemetery,
over two hundred bodies were dissected,

studied for this one rendering—a first
and last communion with sculptor and surgeon

in the bright tension of a shared studio, the curtain
of their flesh parted also in this mute recital.

4

Both fixed and liquescent, this extreme,
uneasy perfection can never forget

itself the way bronze, granite, marble forget;
this demands greater, almost human care—eager

as it is to reject the suspense of exacting form
and return to the possibilities of motion.